To each and every EXPERT—to those parents, grandparents, teachers, librarians, caregivers, child development specialists, pediatricians, nurses, child psychologists and psychoanalysts, health educators, and clergy who read over and looked over our work, talked to us, taught us, and corrected us over and over again as we created this book for young children. We could not have created this book without you. THANK YOU!—R. H. H.

For the love of Becky, as always
N. B. W.

Text copyright © 2011 by Bee Productions, Inc.
Illustrations copyright © 2011 by Nadine Bernard Westcott

First edition 2011

Library of Congress Cataloging-in-Publication Data

Harris, Robie H.
Who has what? : all about girls' bodies and boys' bodies / Robie H. Harris ;
illustrated by Nadine Bernard Westcott.
p. cm. – (Let's Talk About You and Me ; v. 1)
ISBN 978-0-7636-2931-1
1. Sex differences – Juvenile literature. 2. Sex instruction for children.
3. Human body – Juvenile literature. I. Westcott, Nadine Bernard. II. Title. III. Series.
HQ53.H373 2011
612.6 – dc22   2010040464

21 22 23 CCP 15 14
Printed in Shenzhen, Guangdong, China

This book was typeset in Berkeley Old Style.
The illustrations were created digitally.

Candlewick Press
99 Dover Street
Somerville, Massachusetts 02144

visit us at www.candlewick.com

Who Has What?

All About
Girls' Bodies and Boys' Bodies

Robie H. Harris

illustrated by Nadine Bernard Westcott

CANDLEWICK PRESS

Everybody everywhere has a body!

Even babies have bodies—little bodies. When babies' bodies grow bigger, they become kids. When kids' bodies grow bigger, they become grown-ups.

Baby girls and baby boys are born with mostly, but not all, the same body parts.

But most things about boys and girls are the same.
Boys and girls like to catch frogs, swing high up
in the air, ride scooters, and make a lot of noise.

Girls and boys like to run fast, play catch, and take their dollies and stuffed animals for a stroll. And when they get a boo-boo, boys and girls cry. When they do something silly, girls and boys giggle and laugh.

Every boy has a body. Every girl has a body. Every grown-up has a body.

Girls, boys, men, women, mommies, daddies, sisters, brothers, cousins, aunts, uncles, grandmas, grandpas, friends—everywhere you look, everywhere you go, every person has a body!

Boys' and men's bodies have some parts that girls' and women's bodies do not have. Girls' and women's bodies have some parts that boys' and men's bodies do not have. But girls' and boys' bodies are still mostly the same.

Boys and girls have one head, two eyes, two ears,
two cheeks, one nose, one mouth, and one chin.
So do women and men. And so do babies.

Girls and boys have one neck, two shoulders, two arms, two elbows, two wrists, two hands, and ten fingers—two are thumbs and two are pinkies.
So do men and women. And so do babies.

nipple

nipple

waist

bottom

chest

back

knee

knee

leg

tummy

leg

toes

foot

foot

heel

heel

toes

Boys and girls have one chest, two nipples, one waist, one tummy, one bellybutton, one back, one bottom— two legs, two knees, two feet, two heels, and ten toes. So do women and men. And so do babies.

Puppies have a bellybutton. And so do I!

me, too!

bellybutton

bellybutton

Between their legs, girls, baby girls, and women have three openings. They have an opening where pee comes out, an opening to the vagina, and an opening where poop comes out.

But baby boys are not born with an opening to the vagina.

Between their legs, boys, baby boys, and men have a penis, a scrotum, and two openings. They have an opening at the end of the penis where pee comes out and an opening where poop comes out.

But baby girls are not born with a penis or a scrotum.

ovary

ovary

uterus

vagina

Inside their bodies, girls, baby girls, and women have a vagina, a uterus, and two ovaries.

But baby boys are not born with a vagina, or a uterus, or ovaries.

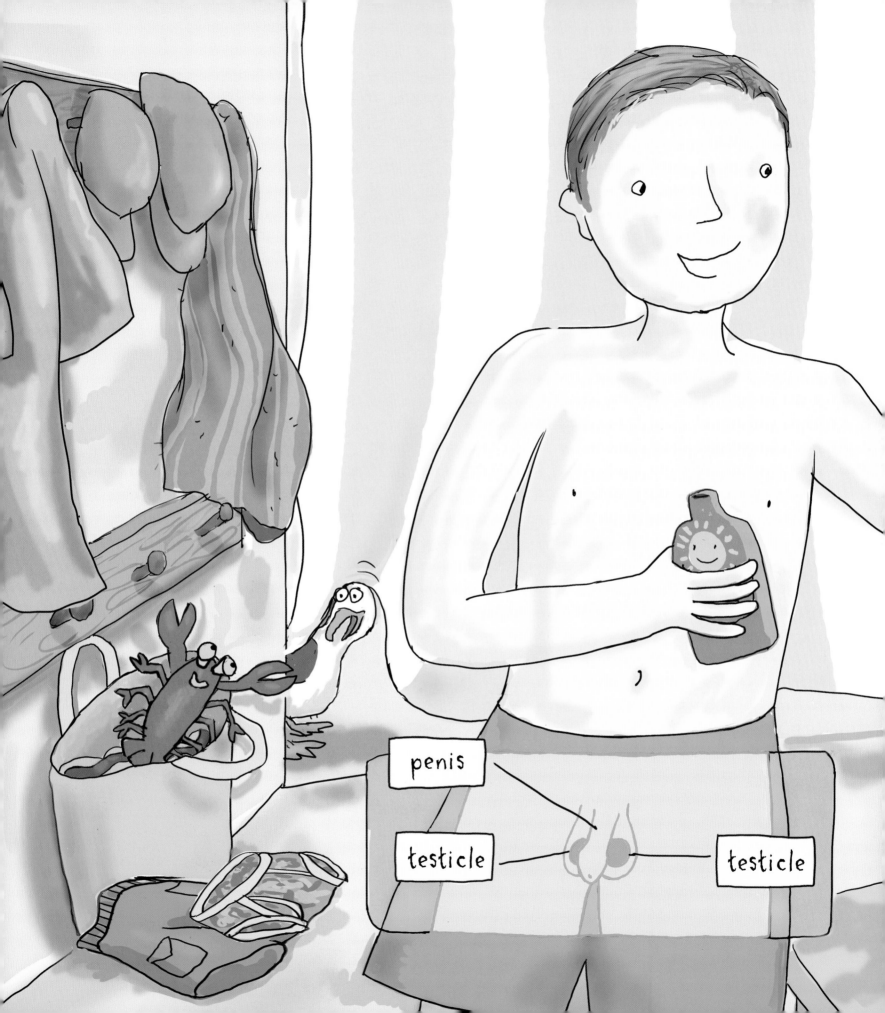

Inside their bodies, boys, baby boys, and men have two testicles. The testicles are inside the scrotum and next to the penis.

But baby girls are not born with testicles.

When girls grow up and become women, the uterus is where a baby can grow until it is born.

After a baby is born, a woman can feed the baby milk from her breasts—or breast milk or formula from a bottle.

When girls grow up—they can become mommies.

When boys grow up and become men, whiskers grow on their faces. Some men have beards or mustaches on their faces. After a baby is born, a man or woman can feed the baby either breast milk from a bottle or formula from a bottle. When boys grow up—they can become daddies.

No matter what kind of body you have—a girl's body or a boy's body, or whatever shape, shade, or size body you have—there is no other body in the whole world just exactly like your body.

And being you is what makes you so wonderful and so special!

Boys and girls keep on growing up and up
until they are grown-ups. Growing from a baby
to a kid to a grown-up takes a long, long, long time.
But as you grow older, you and your body will
still be so awesome, so strong—and so amazing!